THE HOLLOW BONE

IAN MARRIOTT

INDEPENDENT INNOVATIVE INTERNATIONAL

Published by Cinnamon Press
Meirion House
Tanygrisiau
Blaenau Ffestiniog
Gwynedd, LL41 3SU
www.cinnamonpress.com

The right of Ian Marriott to be identified as author of this work has been asserted by him in accordance with the Copyright, Designs and Patent Act, 1988. Copyright © 2017 Ian Marriott
ISBN: 978-1-910836-68-2
British Library Cataloguing in Publication Data. A CIP record for this book can be obtained from the British Library.

Designed and typeset in Palatino by Cinnamon Press. Printed in Poland.
Cover design by Adam Craig from original artwork, 'Bird Skeleton' by © Dannyphoto80, Dreamstime.com
Cinnamon Press is represented in the UK by Inpress Ltd and in Wales by the Welsh Books Council.

Acknowledgements

My thanks to Margaret Gillies Brown and Carol Pope for their kindness and encouragement. To my UEA tutors Denise Riley and George Szirtes for incisive guidance, and, in more recent years, to all at the MBC poetry group for their friendship and critical support. And a special mention to both Dave Evans and Paul Francis.

Acknowledgements are due to the magazines *Urthona* and *Envoi*, and the anthologies *From the City* and *Gazing at Gaia*.

Contents

for my mother and father

The Hollow Bone

Bovine

as if it were not enough
to reduce
the great wild Aurochs
to this swaying udder,
drained twice daily—

I am tired of staring
into dead-eyed water,
bovine water—
all channelled and chained.

Give me the wild water
any day—
a colt of a river,
running over rock—
unfettered, unbroken
from end
to end.

The Half-drowned Valley

An Indian summer.
The levels are down

and an old stone wall,
lost for years, rises
to just beneath the surface.

Hidden,
like an unquiet thought,
and would have remained so
except for a perfect line
of cormorants
using it as a sunning post—

feet planted
on the sunken stone,
wings outstretched like votive gods.

*

And it is often like this—
revelation by proxy.

Quieten the mind
and the old levels
rise up,
to be seen for what they are—

Victorian architecture,
lines of desire
channelled to industry,
locked in stone.

Or desire shunted
into its siding,
awaiting
the engine's return.

*

The sadness of water
is not its lack of home,

but being asked to stay
where it does not belong.

Bridging the Forth

and one day
you set off
alone, to walk—
just for the hell of it!—
from one end
of the bridge
to the other
and back,
without making landfall.

*

The bridge
itself,

all plate and cable
painted for weather,

strung out of tune
to the river hum—

steel cathedral
striding its estuary firth.

*

But far below
the seal's home, the siren home—

tide tugging
a boat-slip moon.

And there is no boatman
to ferry the living

across the shifting river—
only this un-tolled crossing now.

Nose to bumper, bumper to nose—
all those queuing souls…

The slack sail
waits to be filled.

Christmas

Tired
of the absence of god,
the emptiness of words,
we head out early
onto the high moor,
the whole day through thick mist
and deep, untrodden snow.

A whole day without words—
except to share
the whiteness of hares,
grouse flushed up,
a dipper working his watery patch.

It would have been
map and compass work
all morning—and tricky at that—
save for the sure-footed
prints of a fox.

And what a gift—
to come across
this recent absence
making its way
across the moorland
before us.

Blind Love

At first the tree
puts down its root,
a long root, a tap root—
clamps the dark nipple,
nursing the very earth.

It is a kind of braille,
this blind love—
hard-mouthed or soft-mouthed—
a Joey
finding his way
to the pouch.

And only after suckling
for weeks,
does the twinned leaf unfurl,
the stem unfurl—

the long-lashed eyelids
open
to the sun.

Imagine

Imagine being
a flocking bird—

a murmuration
of starlings,

or herring
in its tight-packed shoal.

That lifetime of choices
and hand-brake turns—

never quite theirs,
never quite your own.

*

Or the great white bear,
alone on the ice—

a nose for seal
and menstrual blood—

every ounce of self
nursed from the mother,

sunk in the bone.

The Heroic Age

Scott and Amundsen raced
for the pole, but to them
the pole
was no place at all—

just a great emptiness
waiting to be filled
by that white emptiness
carried from home.

Re-seeding the Moor

August.
The air is thick
with heather bees—

purple further
than the eye
can see.

This maze of squares
and burnt ground—

the gamekeeper,
holding his birds
to the moor.

                *

Yet, out of view,
a private grief.

Acre upon acre
of dying ground—

trenched and pitted
as a rain-soaked Somme,

weeping under
the evening sky.

                *

Two hundred years
of acid rain,

and a heart too acrid
for love to seed

without external agency.

Blue

In the rough pasture,
up behind the cattle field,
a sea of bluebells
astonish
the open ground.

Each year
this phantom bloom,
a blue ache —
the ghost of woods
long gone.

*

Like the slow blue
of an old lover
brought on
by a favourite film—

or visit
to the quiet corner
in the park
we used to use, and use.

*

It has been years.
The poultice earth
has drawn its wound,
leaving only this annual
display—

a bruise of bluebells
breaking into sunlight,
then gone.

The Hare

Under the sky
something shifts.

A scoop of mud lifts, hops,
becomes a scoop of mud again.

His ears are too long for this flattening game
and he knows it.

He is the space between
the flat earth and the flat sky—

he must box the clouds
to keep it open.

Before him there was nothing,
after him there will be nothing again—

pure time.
My awkward, running youth.

Wasps

The wasps are coming in
to die—

alone,
or in little groups,
their hard bodies
ponder the glass
slow as Pythagoras
working his theorem.

*

Each waist a drawn snare—
for I know I will find you

curled in some corner,
pit burial of the sink—

perfect comma
to punctuate my morning

The Sandworm

Far out
on the low tide flats—
sun quiet
on the left behind water—

the more you dig
the more he digs

tail end
disappearing—

he will pass the whole beach
through himself
and back

and is only the bait.

A Kind of Passing

(for Aryamati/Olga Kenyon)

And there is no such thing
as a ritual death.

Buddhist. Activist for twenty years—
she stepped out into busy traffic,

mind on the next best thing.

    *

At the woodland burial
freesias woven

into a wicker coffin
before the long lower away.

The tail end
of hurricane Gonzalo

whipped up
a lifetime of leaves,

and Green Tara
chanted

to the receding
silhouette

of a friend.

Less to attract attention,
than assuage a loneliness—

rising and rising
from within.

Soulcraft

(after Bill Plotkin)

1

Up above
the bell chamber calls,
casts its stony silence.

*

We opened into a belfry.
Strange draughts, or maybe

just the chill
of the place.

Those slotted steps
of a thousand feet,

the leaded windows
with their little leaded light.

Past the clock-room
and its ticking self,

the three-strand banister rope,
the man-made distance.

2

It was a cold
Presbyterian morning.

In the torch-lit rafters
row upon row

of wintering butterflies,
magnetised

like iron filings
to some distant north.

*

Or that array
of tracking telescopes

out in the desert —
able to move

as a single being —
scanning their heaven

for any trace
of an inner hum.

Burnfoot

(for B.D.)

1

The river has eaten a whole field of grazing since you came.
Each year martins loop deeper into the bank.

Your husband squeezes a living from cattle and sheep—
cold mornings nursing tractors, bullying animals out of the mud.

He brought you the lightning struck ash in the top field
burning itself to a stump—

the crossbill plucked from your car radiator
between finger and thumb.

In the quiet corner
otter tracks lead to three dead trout—

his hands soft-mouthed otters
pulling sighs from the bedroom dark.

2

The river is up with season,
white fields drain to black —

your west gable grapples with wind —
in the night a whole cow swept past.

*

Outside
something tests the window,
lifts the latch, and you —
bolt upright, breathing hard,
sentry the dark.

*

But now you sense a soft returning,
something is nosing under the moor —

the urgency of salmon
thrills you, sleepless and breathless

as you run to the river
in nightdress and Wellingtons —

fixed by a strip of stars.

Borderlands

The yearling wolf
sniffed and sprung
its baited trap—

eloped
into his own distance—

without
a backward glance.

The Migration of Caribou

And what of the caribou
on their northern slope—
born to run beside the mother
as her mother before.

Each spring
a river of knowing—
flooding the tundra,
the cotton grass slopes,

until in the end
it's all there is—
this hunger for elsewhere,
the birthing grounds,

forgotten completely
the skin she was born to—
a woman swimming
to reach her own bank.

The Silence

Evening, and the deer
are making their way through the trees—

white rumps bobbing lightly,
coats the colour of spent leaves.

There are couples and dog walkers
lost in a world of their own noise—

but the silence of deer
goes largely un-heard,

knee-deep in the river
drinking their fill.

Woodcock

Shyness
is a woodcock
on her woodland floor.

She has found a way
to be
in this world—
shot-through with humans,
straining their leashes
of sound.

Invisible to all
but those that can see,
I almost stepped on her twice—

though each time
she shuffled away,
stopped, turned,
watched me aslant
with that leaf-coloured eye,

her steadfast refusal
to break into flight.

The Cuckoo

born into that surrogate nest
will never know its real parents.

His is an instinct to scorch and burn,
tipping siblings from the rim of the world,
until newly fledged he flies to Africa—

two-tone loner down to the bone,
avenging something
he may never understand,
that absent father before him.

A Vision of Sheep

Hemmed in by fear,
the tyranny of dogs,

there is little now
between the killing weight
and that long-suckled teat.

Except, perhaps,
the strangeness of deer
appearing and disappearing
like some fleet-footed Hermes
in a twilit corner of the field.

Victoriana

1

Old money,
cold hearth —

the nursemaid provides
a little warmth.

2

In the oak-panelled library
the butterfly collector

opens
his long drawer of lives.

3

There was a little chimney sweep,
who choked to death on soot —

they sent his little brother up
to try and get him oot.

This Central Imperfection

A raindrop gathers
round its grain of dust—

the pearl's hidden
nimbus of grit.

*

Beauty and pain
fused together,

all the better for it.

Pilgrim

These steps are worn,
I am not first,
many others
have passed before—

pious, kneeling,
or lying lengthways
like the barefoot Lama
rounding his mountain,

though in the end
it is much the same,
an arrival at a doorway
lost in the telling—

this opening
into the heart.

The Shaman Speaks

This is not a god
of consolation,
there will be no passage
to the pearly gates –

just one foot planted
more firmly in this world,
and an ache to hear
the call of your twin.

Antarctic Winter 1

Each morning's bruised rim is painful to touch.

Sky-stretched evenings
colour beautifully to blood.

Daylight shrunk
to the moon's unfathomable clock.

Brittle noises in the wind-gapped dark.
Brilliant sunsets are gone.

*

The world fluid has drained out and left us
unprepared for this capillary cold.

I think of those bronze statues left out
to the great Russian winter.

Lead-anchored movement.
Vital organs hoarded away.

Cold cataracts the glazed eye.
The sea has snapped shut.

Antarctic Winter 2

We are anchored by steel.
We are wrapped in fibreglass, sheltered by alien fibres.
We are cocooned in feathers.
We are muffled by fur.
We are living in treacle.
We are living in treacle.
We are managing to cope with these physical improbabilities.

*

But the underarm smell of my mother
carries like a pang over the snow and ocean.

My father's awkward advances
cut keener than this chill wind.

The memory of a woman
knots me as she un-knots me.

I am a Gordian bundle of bone and muscle.

Icebergs

Every schoolboy worth his salt
knows nine-tenths of an iceberg
lies beneath the surface.

The passengers, the galley staff, the whole crew
of the Titanic knew
for that waterlogged instant

the difference between seeing and knowing
that has always troubled

as I stumble knowledgeably
along the path I did not choose

Aurora Landscape

Stars peer.
The crab moon has crawled behind his rock.

Sun left with her hair flailing—

the dumb glass blower
empties his long lungs
of light.

Terra Infirma

Day and night black Pluto's door stands open.
But to retrace your steps and get back to upper air
This is the real task and the real undertaking.

Aeneid, Book VI
Translated by Seamus Heaney

Polar exploration is at once the cleanest and most isolated way of having
a bad time which has been devised.

The Worst Journey in the World
by Apsley Cherry-Garrard

1

Far to the north a forest fire blazes
without any heat.

Bone-white the moon's climbing formaldehyde—
this jar of a place.

2

The blizzard paperweight sits.
Snow settles.
Even the moon is trying to freeze.

3

Fist-in-front-of-face-dark.
Stretching out, the polar night—

between buildings
we cling to ropes of frost.

4

Hand over hand
the deep-sea diver
steady against the bends.

5

Each year the snorkel parka taking its toll at junctions.

6

Night flaps its broken tent.
A porthole moon
peers down
over small inland lakes.

Under the skin it tugs—
slightly parted the harbour mouth.

7

The armadillo sleeps
in its armour of frost—

desire lifts its manhole cover...

or is it
that the knotted umbilicus slips—
needle threading its own navel eye.

8

Out there the suicide principle sits—
he has dropped his long line of hooks
through a hole in the ice and will wait.

9

Up above the listening rod,
horse-hair dark,
frost hieroglyphs the pyramid wall—

beneath floorboards
scarab beetles crawl—

the mummy bags wait—

Sarcophagus of frost.
10

Long held
the tuning forked silence.

Steel cables hum—
whole buildings—
the little body deep in its cubicle sleep.

11

Night-selves play Chinese whispers
through the air conditioning ducts—

who am I this pitch-bright morning
battling the green eyed clock?

The cook, the radio operator—
the Very Low Frequency Engineer
alone in his listening box.

12

Hungrily the moon-owl quarters,
blunt bergs plough through fog.

Wind has put on boots and a whip—
she has locked the door and is coming.

13

The mirage season is on us,
language detaches itself—

deep down the steering mountain
granite horizons waver and lift—

Fata Morgana,
soufflé hills —
the tethered Zeppelin berg.

14

Cook used the last lime a week ago,
salt beef sunsets are gone.

We are down to a hardtack moon,
the weevil holes of stars —
even the weevils themselves —

any gap and we're out
scratting the ground for crumbs of light.

15

Inside the blizzard paperweight we sit.
Wind plays solitaire —
nothing has moved for months.

16

On the night train
truths smuggled
deep across the border —

strapped to his wrist
the locked briefcase of sleep.

17

Noon opens slightly
its sea ice distance —
the livid iris peers and shuts.

Lead thick sea,
black leads invite entrance.

18

The Worst Journey in the World
says it all in those few, awful words—

Burberry and bluster against the cold,
jokes to ward the evil dark—

and all for a penguin's egg
its lizard remains inherent in the yolk.

19

Fish-plump and oily they come,
one-by-one
peeling the sea-ice distance—

heads bowed, each foot
shackled to the press-gang dark.

Cold heron moot,
the magnificent war veteran—
old bees
swarm their hives of frost.

Back bent to the communal winter,
black inward eye,
the oiled key turns

slow as Russia—
a lung of birds,
each on his Faberge´ egg.

20

Between me and you the elevator shaft of sleep—
dream reek rises.

Under the world a swell—
we wait the calving sea.

21

Midwinter.

Picked clean
the skull sits—

a worry of pressure—

cracked fontanel,
the glacier brow
ploughs its forehead dark.

22

Or under the pillow an open crevasse.
Cold-lie detector,
blue-green guillotine negative—

pond-skater of the frozen places,
we will sledge the minefields of frost.

23

Out there
sea-lung exhales—
open leads cloud the mirror glass.

Ice flowers bloom

cold consolation—
frost grows unattended—
slow as truths
or hair
on the laid out dead.

24

25

Shhh!
Put your ear to the low seal hole—
can you hear him
singing his way to the surface?

Now he is out
a bag of seal
lying in the pool of himself.

26

Far to the north a forest fire blazes
giving a little heat—

out on the sea ice distance
the dumb archetypes sit—

flightless and nameless,
backs bent Benedictine—

a worry of birds.

27

Fat from her winter
in the very real element
she comes—

swaggering empress negative—

she will call to her mate
on his nest of frost.

*

Across the fanfare
twilight

each gold throat
trumpets its lost and found.

*

The yolk is devoured
by its albumen moon—

egg-tooth tap-tapping
the bright unknown.

The Ear Shell

after the Maggi Hambling sculpture to Benjamin Britten on Aldburgh Beach

And what is the sea
but me really listening –
or is there another
beyond the pacing ships?

*

Flying fish off the starboard bow,
little iron slivers of sea –

*

Storm waves
days ahead
of the mother event –

or the boat-wake's
slowly widening absence.

*

Island atoll
crusting over
the dead remains
of its first hard thought.

*

Inside
its harbour mouth

the breakwater skull
laps against itself.

Temperate Concerns

1

I have seen the great white bear
tending geraniums
in its balmy northern summer –

last year, a long-toothed narwhal
rang horseshoes
at our annual village fete.

2

The leopard seal
flenses its victim
with a gap-toothed grin –

and the stinking petrel,
neck-deep in blubber –
going for the liver.

The Inner Work

Nearly forty years,
scratching a living
of meat and offal.

Lean pickings
dropped from above—

the mahogany twilight
a half-opened
coffin lid.

*

Then the real hunger.
The work begins.

That whole, un-whole decade
lost beneath the waves—

like the rag-doll seal
of the killer whale—

limp-bodied,
playing dead,

yet all the while
quietly gathering.

The jaws'
careless release.

Strange

At low tide
inking across the limpid pool
I thought I'd taken your measure,

but years later we met again
and nothing could have been
further from the truth—

with your parrot's beak
and eight-legged intelligence
morphing through

that rusted port-hole
so impossibly
smaller than yourself.

And it wasn't the fact
that you'd done it at all,
but the way

you'd gone about the task—
I put it somewhere between
magician and master craftsman,

slowly turning
through the Rubik of your body—
until, with a flick of a wrist

you're through—
gathering together on the other side,
this place too strange to fathom.

The Wild

Careful and deadly,
the wolf pack
dead-woods
its native elk—

gardener snipping
captive roses—
great white secateurs
prune hard back.

*

It is a fact
that the wild
and the tame
do not mix.

Fox in its hen-house
drunk on hens—
wolf amok
in a ranchers yard—

a deer high-tailing
the strangeness of sheep—
or the mind writhing
in its sack of sleep.

Glen Lednock Dam

Far above the last intake
for the hydro-electric,
the dry sluices
and their measuring poles—

I have walked all day
from the valley floor,
to make my peace
with eagle and raven—

with the hare hurrying
from home to home.

     *

Above the mean-ness of man
with his levelling hand—
that bondage of water—
need for control.

Notes on Dochart Falls

1

Water rushes
by the hotel window—
a Victorian cataract
drawing its crowds.

2

Each night
I wake at 3 am,
dreaming of water.
Nice dreams, no drowning.

3

In the evening a gang of kids
crowd against the wall—
they are off their faces
on something modern.

The Cathedrals are Sinking

For six years
the deep-sea diver William Walker
worked alone, in peaty darkness,
to shore the walls of Winchester up—

as masonry tumbled on a dwindling flock,
owls hooted from widening cracks.

                    *

And even today
the un-pinned crypt
will flood heavily
during rainy months—

Antony Gormley
ankle deep
pondering our lot—

or is it simply
that the wet earth
is rising up—

shunned goddess
of cave and fen
reclaiming—without malice—
what was hers
all along.

Summer Geese

The tundra grass is coming to an end,
summer geese have cropped their fill—

there is little here to hold them now,
the empty nest of autumn comes.

This land-locked soul is blown away,
the rush of leaving, overhead.

The Vessel

1

If you don't hit it before
it shits, then you've missed,
is the perceived wisdom
for shooting snipe.

Even when shocked, a bird's
urge to lighten its load
before taking flight.

2

The pregnant hind crosses her stream,
two little ones swimming inside.
And if the Scottish winter
proves too severe,
she will fold one back
into the warmth of herself—
give the other a fighting chance.

3

Bodily choices.
The mind a mad captain, locked in his cabin—
as the river pilot, slipped aboard
on a high-moon tide, steers the vessel
quietly to shore.

The Hollow Bone

Albatross

Sometimes a whole year may pass
between landfall—

green-eyed, glass-eyed
from where you have been,
each iris an ocean trench.

Arctic Tern

For some, home,
is less a place
than sense of becoming,

Bullfinches

Pink gods in winter trees -
or are they working the orchard clean?

Dipper

In and out
of the black river,

eating darkness
to bring new life.

Heron

Each forward movement an age—
the eyes' fixed bayonet.

House martin

That rank reality
of mud and spit—

two beings
and a desperate joy

weaving
the vertical earth.

Seagull

Land lubber, refuse stalker,
the sea's rebuff—

each flight your cold feet
will send you back.

Snow petrel (dead)

This weightless body
a feather in the palm—

within her bones
the soul of a land.

Woodpecker

The skin of a walrus
stretched over bone —

Eliot under
an Inuit moon.

*

A crack
in the language
to let light in—

or the woodpecker
drumming his place
in the world.

The Dream Master

A lone man
hauls his sledge
over the plateau rim—

meeting himself head-on,
is unable to speak for weeks.

*

Up and out at dawn,
tip-toeing crevasse-fields
in the slanting light,
daytime-darkness rising.

And there is no map
for the shifting ice—

just east-south-east
on a dream bearing,
a month of supplies for one.

*

But who is the dream master?
Two-faced Janus staring out,

or the all-powerful Oz,
booming instructions
through his homesick
curtain of sleep.

*

Up here
over half the world
is weather—
an approaching storm
the child's tantrum
tearing up its page.